FROM CATERPILLAR TO BUTTERFLY

Anita Ganeri

Heinemann
LIBRARY

www.heinemann.co.uk/library

Visit our website to find out more information about Heinemann Library books.

To order:

 Phone 44 (0) 1865 888066

 Send a fax to 44 (0) 1865 314091

 Visit the Heinemann Bookshop at www.heinemann.co.uk/library to browse our catalogue and order online.

First published in Great Britain by Heinemann Library, Halley Court, Jordan Hill, Oxford OX2 8EJ, part of Harcourt Education. Heinemann is a registered trademark of Harcourt Education Ltd.

Editorial: Nancy Dickmann and Sarah Chappelow
Design: Ron Kamen and edesign
Picture Research: Ruth Blair and Kay Altwegg
Production: Helen McCreath

Originated by Modern Age
Printed and bound in China by South China Printing Company

13 digit ISBN 978 0 4310 5072 0 (HB)
10 digit ISBN 0 4310 5072 4 (HB)
10 09 08 07 06
10 9 8 7 6 5 4 3 2 1

13 digit ISBN 978 0 4310 5082 9 (PB)
10 digit ISBN 0 4310 5082 1 (PB)
11 10 09 08 07
10 9 8 7 6 5 4 3 2 1

The British Library Cataloguing in Publication Data
Ganeri, Anita
From caterpillar to butterfly. - (How living things grow)
571.8'15789
A full catalogue record for this book is available from the British Library.

Acknowledgements
The Publishers would like to thank the following for permission to reproduce the following photographs: Alamy pp. 9, 10, 18, 19, 24 (Robert M. Vera), 26, 27, 29 (Jill Stephenson); Ardea p. 20 (Francois Gohier); Corbis pp. 6 (George D. Lepp), 29 (Michael & Patricia Fogden); FLPA pp. 11 (S & D & K Maslowski), 13 (Dembinsky Photo Ass.), 14 (Tom and Pam Gardner), 22 (Frans Lanting/Minden Pictures), 23 (Frans Lanting/Minden Pictures); Naturepl.com p. 5 (Tom Vezo); NHPA p. 4 (Stephen Dalton), 12 (Rod Planck). 15 (T Kitchin & V Hurst), 16 (T Kitchin & V Hurst), 17 (T Kitchin & V Hurst), 25 (Stephen Dalton); Oxford Scientific Library p. 7; Photolibrary.com p. 8. Cover photograph of a butterfly reproduced with permission of NHPA/Stephen Dalton.

Illustrations: Martin Sanders

The Publishers would like to thank Michael Scott for his assistance in the preparation of this book.

Every effort has been made to contact copyright holders of any material reproduced in this book. Any omissions will be rectified in subsequent printings if notice is given to the publishers. The paper used to print this book comes from sustainable resources.

Contents

Words written in bold, **like this**, are explained in the glossary.

Have you ever seen
a butterfly?

Butterflies live all over the world.
There are many kinds of butterflies.
A butterfly is a type of **insect**.

A butterfly has two pairs of wings, two **antennae** and three pairs of legs.

You are going to learn about a Monarch butterfly. You will learn how a Monarch butterfly is born, grows up, has babies, gets old, and dies. This is the butterfly's life cycle.

How does the butterfly's life cycle start?

5

Butterfly eggs

The butterfly starts life as a tiny egg. A female butterfly lays the eggs in summer. She lays hundreds of eggs on the leaves of a **milkweed** plant.

The female lays her eggs, then she flies away.

*Each egg is about
as big as a grain of rice.*

The little eggs are white and
oval-shaped. They have small
grooves running down the sides.

What happens
to the eggs?

Hungry caterpillars

About four days later, the eggs start to **hatch**. There is a little **caterpillar** in each egg. The caterpillar chews a hole in its egg.

Squeezing out of the egg is hard work.

The caterpillar is hungry!
First, it eats up its eggshell.
Then it starts to munch the
juicy **milkweed** leaves.

The caterpillar spends all day eating.

Warning stripes

A Monarch **caterpillar** has yellow, white, and black stripes. They warn birds that the caterpillar is **poisonous**!

These bright colours are hard to miss.

Birds like to eat green caterpillars like this one.
But they keep away from caterpillars with stripes.

The caterpillar gets its poison from
the **milkweed** leaves it eats.
The leaves have a juice in them
that makes the caterpillar
taste nasty.

How quickly does the
caterpillar grow?

Growing bigger

The **caterpillar** grows very quickly but its outer skin does not grow. Soon its skin gets so tight that it splits open and falls off.

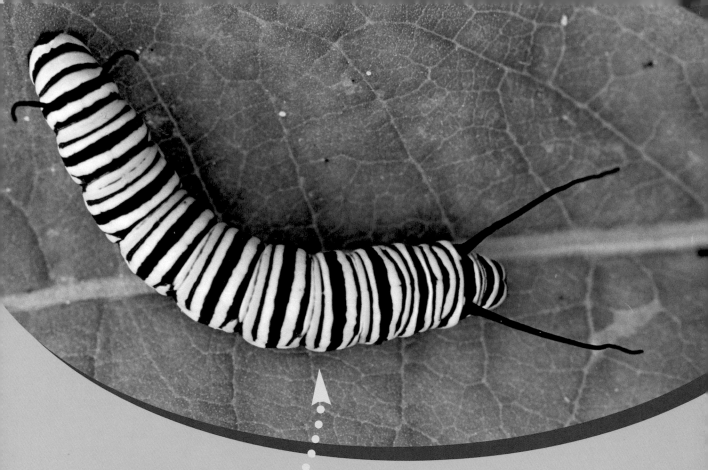

The caterpillar is fully grown and ready for the next stage of its life.

The caterpillar has a new, stretchy skin under its old one. It changes its skin this way four or five times as it grows. This is called **moulting**.

A tough case

It is two weeks after the **caterpillar hatched**. Now it has reached its full size. It hangs upside-down from a leaf or twig. Then its stripy skin splits for the last time.

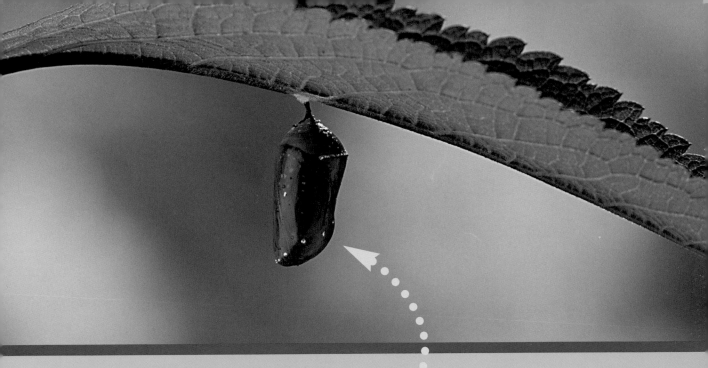

Inside the chrysalis the caterpillar begins to change.

There is a hard case under this skin. This case is called a **chrysalis**. It is green and gold. The chrysalis keeps the caterpillar safe inside.

How does the caterpillar change into a butterfly?

Beautiful butterfly

The **caterpillar's** body changes inside the **chrysalis**. It turns into a butterfly. This takes about ten days. Then the chrysalis splits open. A butterfly wriggles out.

It takes the butterfly about an hour to get out of the chrysalis.

The new butterfly holds its wings out so that they dry.

At first, the butterfly's wings are soft and damp. They soon dry and go hard. The beautiful butterfly is ready to fly away.

What does the butterfly eat?

Flower food

The butterfly eats a sweet
juice made by flowers.
This juice is
called
nectar.

The butterfly sucks up the nectar with its long tongue. Its tongue works like a drinking straw.

The butterfly's long tongue reaches into the flower

19

A long flight

In autumn, it starts to get colder.
The butterfly cannot stand the cold.
If it gets too cold, it will die. Instead,
it gets ready for a very long flight.

*Millions of butterflies
start their long flight.*

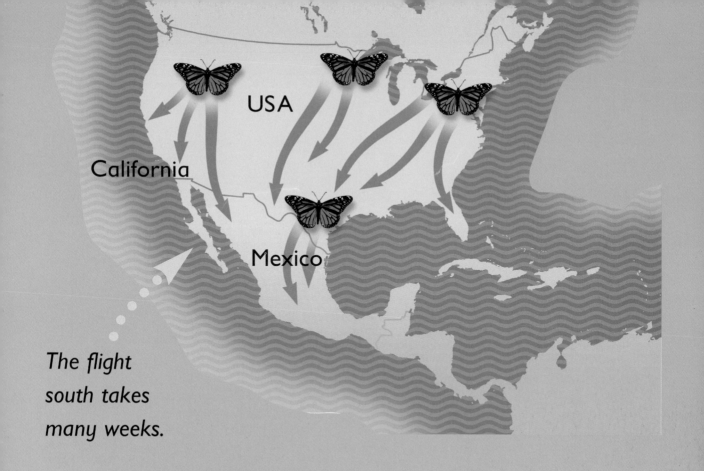

The flight south takes many weeks.

The butterfly flies south to a warmer place. Some butterflies fly to California, USA. Some butterflies fly to Mexico.

What does the butterfly do there?

21

Winter sleep

After its long flight, the butterfly lands on a tree. Then the butterfly goes into a deep sleep for most of the winter. This sleep is called **hibernation**.

Lots of butterflies group together on the branches.

While the butterfly is hibernating, its body works very slowly. This helps it to save **energy**. The butterfly does not eat. It lives off stores of fat in its body.

When does the butterfly wake up?

Waking up

Spring comes and it gets warmer.
The butterfly wakes up from its
sleep. It finds some flowers to feed
on. Then the butterfly starts to
fly back north.

*The butterfly needs **energy**
for the long flight home.*

24

Many butterflies die long before they complete their journey north.

Some male and female butterflies **mate** on the way. Then the female lays her eggs. **Caterpillars hatch** and turn into butterflies. These new butterflies also fly north.

What happens to the butterflies?

More butterflies

When they finish their journey, the butterflies lay more eggs, then they die. The eggs **hatch** into more adult butterflies. These lay more eggs, then they also die.

Some adult butterflies only live for a few weeks.

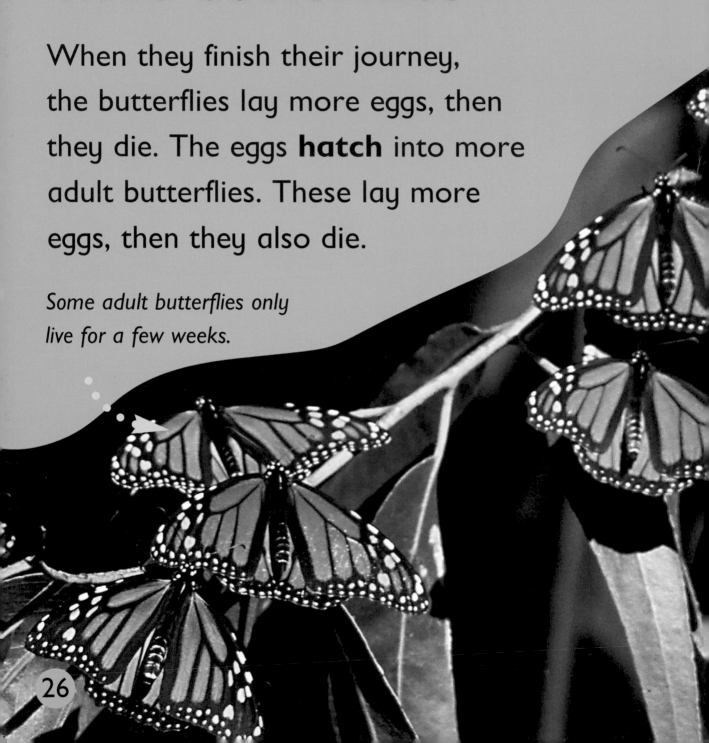

Butterflies that hatch in spring and summer never have to make the long flight south. Their life cycle begins again in the north.

Life cycle of a Monarch butterfly

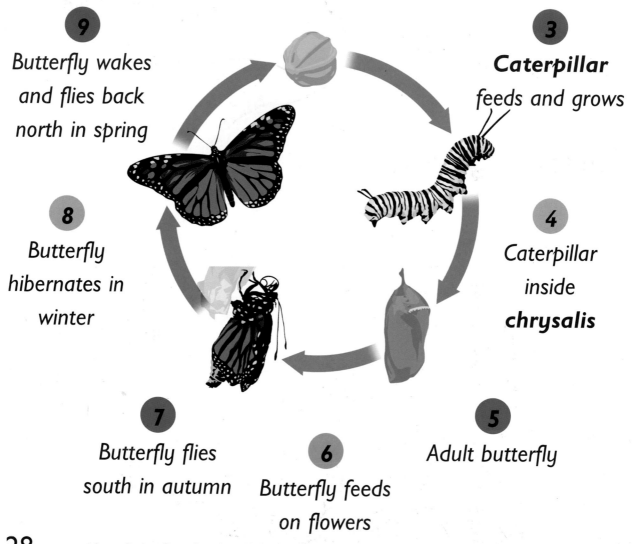

1 Butterfly **mates** and lays eggs

2 Eggs **hatch**

3 **Caterpillar** feeds and grows

4 Caterpillar inside **chrysalis**

5 Adult butterfly

6 Butterfly feeds on flowers

7 Butterfly flies south in autumn

8 Butterfly hibernates in winter

9 Butterfly wakes and flies back north in spring

Note: Butterflies that hatch in spring and summer miss out stages 7, 8, and 9.

Caterpillar map

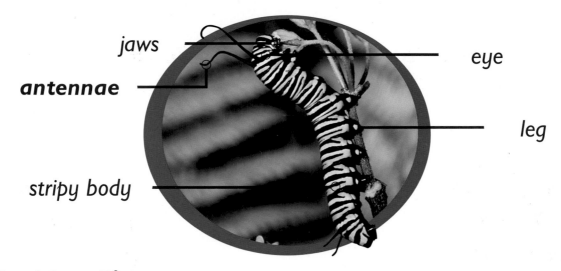

jaws

antennae

eye

leg

stripy body

Butterfly map

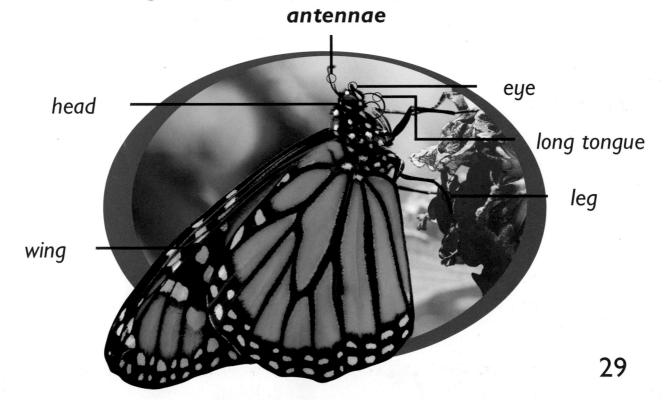

antennae

head

eye

long tongue

leg

wing

29

Glossary

antennae feelers on an insect's head

caterpillar young butterfly which hatches out of an egg

chrysalis hard case which grows around a caterpillar

energy power needed for an animal's body to work

hatch to break out of an egg

hibernation deep sleep over winter

insect animal with six legs like a butterfly

mate when a male and female animal come together to make young

milkweed kind of plant with pink flowers that grows in North America

moulting when an animal's old skin falls off and a new skin grows underneath

nectar sweet juice made in a flower

oval-shaped shaped like a squashed circle

poisonous full of juice that is nasty or dangerous to eat

More books to read

Life Cycle of a Butterfly, Angela Royston
  (Heinemann Library, 2001)

Life Cycles: Butterfly, Louise Spilsbury
  (Heinemann Library, 2003)

Nature's Patterns: Animal Life Cycles, Anita Ganeri
  (Heinemann Library, 2005)

Websites to visit

Visit these websites to find out more interesting facts about Monarch butterflies:

http://www.monarchwatch.org

http://www.monarchbutterflyusa.com

Index